What's in this book

学习内容 Contents   2

读一读 Read   4

听听说说 Listen and say   12

写一写 Write   16

多元学习 Connections   18

温习 Checkpoint   20

分享 Sharing   22

This book belongs to

_____

音乐家莫扎特
The musician Mozart

学习内容 Contents

沟通 Communication

说出乐器名称
Say the names of some musical instruments

说说音乐家莫扎特
Talk about the great musician Mozart

生词 New words

⭐ 音乐	music
⭐ 拉	to play
⭐ 小提琴	violin
⭐ 聪明	clever
⭐ 容易	easy
⭐ 难	difficult
⭐ 礼物	present
⭐ 小时候	when I was small
⭐ 小时	hour
⭐ 正在	while, in the process of
钢琴	piano
弹	to play
歌剧	opera

姐姐正在弹钢琴。

My sister is playing the piano.

文化 Cultures

认识中国乐器

Learn about Chinese musical instruments

跨学科学习 Project

认识声音是如何产生的，制作水杯木琴

Learn how sound is produced and make a water glass xylophone

Get ready

1 Do you like classical music?

2 Do you know the people in the pictures?

3 Have you heard any music composed by Mozart?

你知道莫扎特吗？他很聪明，在他
小时候，人们都叫他音乐神童。

有一天，姐姐正在弹钢琴，他在旁
边看，学会了容易的曲子。

莫扎特很努力，每天弹几个小时钢琴，很快就会弹很难的曲子。

他还跟爸爸学习拉小提琴。十几岁的时候，他就写了第一部歌剧。

莫扎特写了很多优秀的作品，他在各地的表演也都很成功。

lǐ wù
礼物

莫扎特35岁就去世了。这些作品都是他留给我们的礼物。

Let's think

1 Recall the story. Number the pictures in order.

2 Do you like music? Discuss what music you like and don't like with your friend.

你喜欢音乐吗？
为什么？

我喜欢……
因为……

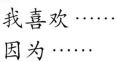

我不喜欢……
因为……

New words

1 Learn the new words.

2 Listen to your teacher and point to the correct words above.

听听说说 Listen and say

04 **2** Look at the pictures. Listen to the story a

1 星期六，浩浩做了什么？

　　a 去爷爷家玩

　　b 去办公室上班

　　c 弹钢琴

2 玲玲去年的生日礼物是什么？

　　a 小提琴

　　b 蛋糕

　　c 钢琴

3 伊森和艾文要做什么？

　　a 听音乐

　　b 看电影

　　c 看歌剧

① 星期五学校音乐节，你们唱歌还是跳舞？

　你等着看伊森、艾文和我的歌剧吧

　你们呢？

　我弹钢琴，姐姐唱歌，还有布朗尼跳舞。

歌剧会不会很难唱？

不太难。伊森和艾文正在音乐室唱歌，我现在也要去那里。

布朗尼会跳舞？它真聪明！

它现在正在跟姐姐一起跳舞呢！

3 Complete the sentences and role-play with your friend.

a 给她打针
b 看报纸　c 刷牙

医生正在做什么？

小女孩生病了，医生正在___。

爷爷和奶奶正在做什么？

爷爷和奶奶正在一起___。

已经七点了，快来吃早饭，上学要迟到了。

我正在___，快好了。

Task

Who is your favourite musician? Do some research and talk about him/her with your friend.

我很喜欢……

Paste your photo here.

他叫莫扎特，他很聪明，十几岁就会写歌剧。今天，还有很多人非常喜欢他的音乐。你听过他写的歌剧吗？我很喜欢。你可以上网去听听。

Game

Play with your friends. Count the number of piano keys below in Chinese. Who can do it faster?

黑色的有多少个？
白色的有多少个？

一、二、三……

……十四、十五、十六……

黑色的有……个，
白色的有……

Chant

莫扎特小神童，
聪明认真无人比，
能拉提琴弹钢琴，
能写歌剧和乐曲。
莫扎特音乐家，
努力优秀又年轻，
世界各地去表演，
留下很多好作品。

生活用语 Daily expressions

真聪明！
So clever!

太难了。
It's so difficult.

15

写一写 Write

1 Trace and write the characters.

丶 亠 亠 产 立 产 音 音 音

丿 仁 与 乒 乐

音	乐	音	乐
音	乐		

一 丅 丅 正 正

一 ナ 才 不 在 在

正	在	正	在
正	在		

2 Write and say.

我很喜欢听＿＿
＿＿，我每天会
听一个小时。

他们是五年级的
学生，＿＿＿＿
教室里考试。

3 Read and circle the correct words.

今天放学后，我和姐姐一起去（音乐室／图书馆）学习拉（提琴／钢琴）。

我和姐姐拉的提琴不一样，我拉大提琴，姐姐拉小提琴。我学习大提琴快半年了，我觉得它很（难／容易）拉，我应该好好学习。姐姐四岁的时候开始学习小提琴，她很（聪明／漂亮），老师新教的音乐，她拉了一个多（小时／小时候）就会了。你想听我和姐姐一起（弹／拉）提琴吗？

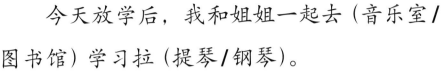
拼音输入法 Pinyin input

Write the letters in the correct blanks to complete the passage.
Then type the whole passage.

| a 中间还写着莫扎特的姓名 | b 更喜欢莫扎特的音乐 | c 还在这里弹琴、写歌剧 |

八月的时候，爸爸带我去参观了莫扎特住过的房子。

这所房子是黄色的，有很多窗户，___。爸爸说，莫扎特住在这里，___。

我很喜欢这所房子，但是我___。

多元学习 Connections

Cultures

1 The traditional Chinese musical instruments usually fall into four types. Learn about them.

The plucked instruments

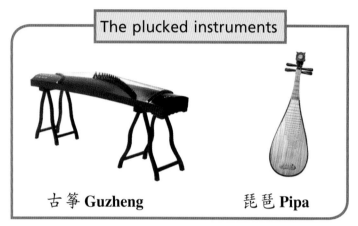

古筝 Guzheng   琵琶 Pipa

The majority of the traditional Chinese instruments are made of wood, bamboo and leather.

Chinese instruments are either played solo, in small ensembles or in large orchestra .

The bowed instruments

二胡 Erhu

The percussion instruments

鼓 Chinese drum

The wind instruments

笛子 Dizi

2 Chinese children usually learn to play traditional music at school. Talk about these pictures with your friend.

她正在弹《赛马》(*Horse Racing*) 这个音乐吗?

我不知道，但是中国音乐很好听，我喜欢。

Project

1 Do you know how sound is produced? Do an experiment and learn about it.

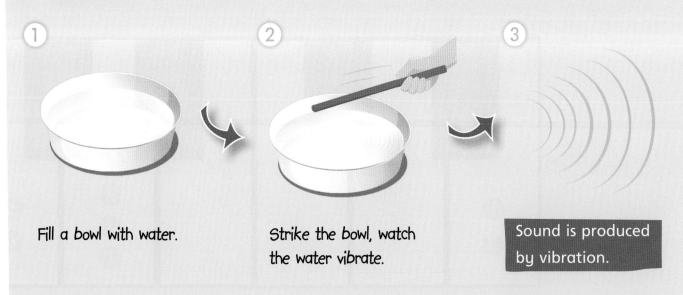

① Fill a bowl with water.

② Strike the bowl, watch the water vibrate.

③ Sound is produced by vibration.

2 Make a water glass xylophone. Perform to your friend.

做音乐不难，很容易！

真好听！真好玩！

温习 Checkpoint

1 Write the characters and say the sentences aloud. Then play the piano keys as numbered. Can you guess which music note you played?

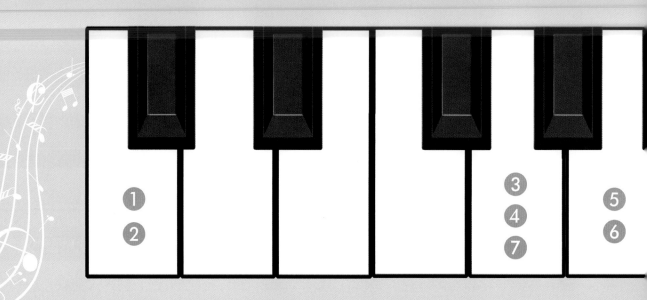

1 你会不会写 music 的中文字？

2 莫扎特正在弹钢琴。

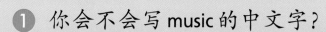

3 我每天听一个小时音乐。

4 这个小提琴是妈妈给我的生日礼物。

5 她很聪明，三岁的时候开始学弹钢琴。

6 明天是星期六，我们一起去看歌剧吧！

7 长大了我也想做莫扎特那样的音乐家。

2 Work with your friend. Colour the stars and the chillies.

Words and sentences			
音乐	☆	☆	☆
拉	☆	☆	🌶
小提琴	☆	☆	🌶
聪明	☆	☆	🌶
容易	☆	☆	🌶
难	☆	☆	🌶
礼物	☆	☆	🌶
小时候	☆	☆	🌶
小时	☆	☆	🌶
正在	☆	☆	☆
钢琴	☆	🌶	🌶
弹	☆	🌶	🌶
歌剧	☆	🌶	🌶
姐姐正在弹钢琴。	☆	☆	🌶

Say the names of some musical instruments	☆
Talk about the great musician Mozart	☆

3 What does your teacher say?

分享 Sharing

Words I remember

音乐	yīn yuè	music
拉	lā	to play
小提琴	xiǎo tí qín	violin
聪明	cōng ming	clever
容易	róng yì	easy
难	nán	difficult
礼物	lǐ wù	present
小时候	xiǎo shí hou	when I was small
小时	xiǎo shí	hour
正在	zhèng zài	while, in the process o
钢琴	gāng qín	piano
弹	tán	to play
歌剧	gē jù	opera

Other words

神童	shén tóng	prodigy
曲子	qǔ zi	melody

努力	nǔ lì	to make efforts
就	jiù	already
跟	gēn	with
部	bù	volume
优秀	yōu xiù	outstanding
作品	zuò pǐn	composition
各地	gè dì	everywhere
表演	biǎo yǎn	performance
成功	chéng gōng	successful
去世	qù shì	to pass away
留	liú	to leave
乐器	yuè qì	musical instruments
古筝	gǔ zhēng	guzheng
琵琶	pí pa	pipa
二胡	èr hú	erhu
鼓	gǔ	Chinese drum
笛子	dí zi	dizi

OXFORD
UNIVERSITY PRESS

Oxford University Press is a department of the University of Oxford.
It furthers the University's objective of excellence in research, scholarship,
and education by publishing worldwide. Oxford is a registered trade mark of
Oxford University Press in the UK and in certain other countries

Published in Hong Kong by
Oxford University Press (China) Limited
39th Floor, One Kowloon, 1 Wang Yuen Street, Kowloon Bay,
Hong Kong

Illustrated by Ah Lun, Anne Lee, Emily Chan, KY Chan and Wildman

Photographs for reproduction permitted by Dreamstime.com

China National Publications Import & Export (Group) Corporation is an authorized distributor of
Oxford Elementary Chinese.

Please contact content@cnpiec.com.cn or 86-10-65856782

ISBN: 978-0-19-082311-5

10 9 8 7 6 5 4 3 2